How to Manage a Consulting Project

Make Money, Get Your Project Done on Time, and Get Referred Again and Again

Richard G Lowe, Jr

How to Manage a Consulting Project

Make Money, Get Your Project Done on Time, and Get Referred Again and Again

Business Professional Series #1

Published by The Writing King
www.thewritingking.com

How to Manage a Consulting Project

Cover Artist: theamateurzone

ASIN: B013MLRIXU
ISBN: 978-1-943517-69-5 (Hardcover)
ISBN: 978-1-943517-68-8 (Paperback)
ISBN: 978-1-943517-10-7 (eBook)

Table of Contents

Table of Contents

Introduction

During my second semester in college, I arrived late at the twice-annual tradition of registration. To my dismay, the good classes were filled, and all that was left were a couple of computer courses with funny sounding names. This was long before computers were cool. In fact, I'd never seen one before and only knew about them from science fiction stories.

I didn't want to take a computer class, but there was nothing left, and I had to fill my schedule. I signed up, and by the end of the first day of the first class I was hooked.

My teacher was a very tall man—almost 7 feet— and very knowledgeable and likable. His name was Fred, and after a single semester I knew what I was going to be doing with the rest of my life.

Near the end of the semester, I was awarded my first consulting gig. This involved correcting some bugs in the general ledger programs that ran on a TRS-80 computer. At the time, this was the most modern machine that could be purchased. It came complete with 16kKB of memory and two 5 ¼ inch floppy disk drives. I was overconfident, underprepared, and very naïve. I had my eye on the $600 that was offered to complete the job and didn't realize that I didn't know how to fix the programs until it was too late.

Looking back on those days, I realize I did everything wrong that I could possibly do wrong. I didn't validate my assumptions, didn't write an SOW, and didn't terminate the contract when I found I was in over my head.

Introduction

Now, 35 years later, I've been a part of or managed over a thousand consulting projects. Some of these were small, lasting an hour or two, some required weeks of labor, and others needed teams of 20 people working for months at a time.

Virtually all these projects were successfully completed relatively close to the budget and almost always on time. I learned there was a certain joy in delivering a service to a client of high quality and that met or exceeded the specifications.

Those projects that didn't go well failed in over 90% of the cases because of poor communications with the client. Conversely, those projects that succeeded did so primarily because of excellent communication between the client, the implementation team, and me.

Good communication starts with the sales effort, continues by writing a high-quality statement of work (SOW), and proceeds all the way to the end of the project with the use of meetings, email, Skype, interviews, and the telephone.

Of course, there are many other factors that go into the success or failure of a project. Obviously, a consultant must be competent and understand the service that he is selling, and must be able to manage and control the chaos that can happen in any activity involving many people.

Change must be managed as well. A project that is otherwise going well can be thoroughly torpedoed and sink into the depths if change is not controlled properly.

In this book, I'll present many of the lessons I learned about how to manage a project from beginning to end. I'll talk about what makes a project go right and the things that can go wrong.

I hope you enjoy what I've written and find it to be of some value. If you would like to send me a note about this book, feel free to write me at rich@thewritingking.com. If you enjoyed the book, please write a positive review.

What is a consulting project?

Congratulations! You've been hired by a client to get something done. Presumably, you have some sort of expertise in the area, you have someone on your team who is knowledgeable, or you'll be hiring somebody who does.

You are trusted, regardless of whether you're being paid five dollars through a freelancing website or tens of thousands of dollars direct from the client. Someone trusts that you have the knowledge and expertise to complete a task within a specified timeframe for a specific amount of money.

It is vital that you uphold that trust. Of course, there are consultants who fail at what they do, overrun their schedules, come in over budget, and do slipshod work. You don't want to be one of those consultants, do you?

When you do a good job, you get recommended. On freelancing websites, the client may give you a good review. When you're working directly with a client, they may give you a testimonial. When one of their friends, peers or co-workers asks for a consultant, if you did a good job they may recommend you. That's the best way to get new business.

On the other hand, when you do a poor job, you may get a bad review or no testimonial. You certainly won't get recommended, and anybody who asked the client about you may get stony silence or a stream of curses. You don't want that, do you?

What is a consulting project?

In the world of marketing, there is nothing more powerful than a personal recommendation from someone. This is true whether you are looking for a job, searching for a consultant, or buying a car.

A recommendation from a trusted source is the most powerful marketing on the planet. All of the positions that I have held throughout my career began because of a recommendation. I never had any luck playing the resume game.

I served as Vice President of Consulting for 14 years. The vast majority of my projects were landed as a result of recommendations from clients. After being a consultant for so long, I landed on the other side of the fence at Trader Joe's and hired hundreds of consultants, virtually always based on recommendations.

When you are a consultant, it is important to remember you are also a salesperson and a marketer. You are always selling the next project, and you are always marketing your services. You do this by being a professional, delivering an excellent product, within budget and on time, managing the project expertly, and communicating at a high level.

At all stages of the project, keep in mind that strong positive recommendations are almost as valuable as cash in the bank. Remember, a solid recommendation from your client means you did a good job.

Your client makes a choice every time a task needs to get done—do it myself (insource) or get someone else to do it (outsource). Sometimes internal policies prejudice that choice. When I was Director of Operations at Trader Joe's, company policy demanded that our staff remain small. This forced us to outsource creatively on a regular basis.

When I was the Vice President of Consulting at Software Techniques, money was tight, and the preference was to do things in house. The general feeling was that outsourcing cost money, thus reduced our profits. As a result, we tended to avoid hiring an external consultant unless there was no choice.

Besides internal policies, another reason why a company or a person looks for a consultant is they don't have the skill set needed to get something done. For example, a ghostwriter might be skilled at writing, but may not have the skills of a graphic artist. The ghost writer may hire an artist to create his book cover.

In fact, a ghostwriter is a consultant who has been hired to write an article or a book. Ghostwriters are often needed because the client doesn't have the writing skills or time needed to do the work.

Of course, time is often the consideration that leads to needing the services of consultants. I've managed many projects where I didn't have the internal staff to complete the work in any reasonable time frame. This required me to look outside for additional resources.

Sometimes consultants are hired to prevent conflicts of interest. For example, companies that accept credit cards are required to get a yearly security audit. Internal staff cannot be used to perform these audits because the conclusions would be biased and not trusted. Thus, an external company who

What is a consulting project?

specializes in security is hired to validate the security controls and write a report.

Statement of work

You must formally define your project, regardless of whether it is just a five dollar gig or requires thousands of man-hours at a cost of millions of dollars. For a gig on a freelancing site, it is often simply a matter of writing a good description of the service you offer.

Normally, you should create a detailed Statement of Work (SOW) for each project that you manage. An SOW is a legal document that describes the project, the relationship between you and the client, payment and termination clauses, and the structure of the effort.

When I first started in the consulting business back in 1981, we didn't create SOW's. There was usually a contract that defined the legal relationship between the client and us, but we virtually never defined the scope of the project in an SOW.

Sometimes you can get away with not having an SOW. I wouldn't recommend it, because it makes it difficult to determine the boundaries of the project.

One of the main purposes of an SOW is to define the project scope. For example, in 1984 we were contracted to create a simple application to take a date in human readable format and translate it into something the machine understood. As the project progressed, the client mentioned he wanted the time added, to have multiple time zones, and to be able to put in relative dates (three days from today or last week, for example).

Statement of work

All of those additions were outside of the original scope of the project. But we didn't create an SOW, so we had a difficult time arguing that these new capabilities were not part of what we were contracted to complete. Thus, a project that is estimated for a few hours became a monster that took a week to finish.

An SOW for this project would've stated the application would accept a human formatted date and convert it to a machine formatted date. Anything the client added after that would have clearly been outside of the scope and would result in an increase in price.

In smaller projects, the statement of work is created as part of the sales effort. The SOW for larger projects, however, may require funding from the client. This is especially true for small consulting companies who cannot afford the resources to fund a detailed SOW for a large project.

Unfortunately, most clients will not pay for the creation of an SOW. The way I handle this conundrum is to define the first phase of the project as an exploratory phase, after which the estimate and timeframe for the rest of the project will be modified and detailed as needed.

You may find it best to split a large project up into multiple SOWs. In other words, create a master SOW, which references smaller subprojects, each with their own SOW. This makes it easier to manage since each individual subproject can be handled separately. It also makes it easier to spot changes in scope which otherwise might be more difficult to spot in a single large project.

For example, if your company was contracted to develop a new furniture warehouse system, you might write a separate SOW for each application that was part of that project. You would then treat each subproject, with its own separate SOW, as a separate project.

DEFINE THE PURPOSE AND DELIVERABLES

Your SOW needs to define the overall purpose of the project. This is generally the first section of the SOW, and it sets the overall scope of the project. Constrain yourself to define the deliverables of the project in this part of the SOW. You are concerned with the end results, not how, when, who, or how much; those come later in the SOW.

For example, the SOW for the project to create a book cover for a novel would state, "The purpose of this project is to create one book cover for the *Alternate Space* novel. This cover shall be suitable for an eBook."

Include bullet points in this section to define individual deliverables.

You can also define exclusions or things that are specifically not delivered. For example, in a ghostwriting project this section would explain the deliverable as a finished novel of 300 pages with a word count of 40,000, and then note that proofreading is not included in the project.

DEFINE THE MONEY

THE ESTIMATE

Within the SOW, you need to define how much the project is going cost. It's quite common that there is not sufficient

Statement of work

information to accurately estimate the project when the SOW was written. This can make it difficult, if not impossible, to quote an accurate cost until later in the project.

After managing hundreds of consulting efforts during my career, I've come to the conclusion that all projects must allow an initial period where assumptions are validated, facts are checked, and analysis is done. This benefits both the client and the consultant and leads to a project that is more likely to succeed.

An old boss of mine had the belief that including the word "estimate" meant that the price could change. Out of the many hundreds of projects that I have delivered as a consultant, not once has the client ever interpreted the word "estimate" in this manner; once a price is quoted, it can be difficult to discuss changes with the client later.

Thus, be more specific and specify that the quote may change once the analysis is complete and assumptions are validated.

Sometimes there is a Catch-22 condition. The client must know the cost of the project before he can approve it. Yet, the consultant cannot quote a price because he has insufficient data and has not had a chance to validate the assumptions.

There are several ways you can structure a project to get around this conundrum. I've listed a few of them below.

Phased approach: In my ghostwriting projects, for example, I define projects using a phased approach. I define the purpose of the first phase as writing the first couple of chapters of the book and defining in detail the remainder of the project. When the first phase is done, the project is re-estimated and, if needed, an adjustment to the price or schedule is made.

Pilot: On larger projects, it is very common to create a pilot program in advance of the main project. This is especially true if something is being developed, as in the case of a new computer application.

Basically, you create a smaller, pilot effort that is completed in advance of the main project. The pilot will have its own SOW distinct and separate from the SOW of the follow-on project. The purpose of the pilot is to validate or define assumptions, risks, estimates, and schedules.

A pilot project should be funded by your client, and it must be treated as distinct and unique from the follow-on project.

Ballpark it: There are times when the client is not willing to fund a pilot or allow the project to be re-estimated after the first phase. This puts a consultant in a difficult position, because most of the data needed to estimate the project is unknown, or worse, is false or based on faulty assumptions.

Most project disasters occur when the client wants a price cast in stone in the SOW without building in a way to adjust the price once the assumptions have been validated, and the data about the project is more fully understood.

Many consultants are faced with this situation. Quite often, their solution is to add a "fudge factor" or a "contingency amount"; this can also be called padding the project.

Statement of work

There are dangers to this approach. By padding, you may price yourself out of reach of your client and thus not be awarded the project. Because you don't know all of the facts and have not validated the assumptions, it is possible even with padding you could exceed the budget.

Be very cautious about accepting a project that doesn't include, in one form or another, a method to adjust the cost and schedule after the facts are known, and assumptions are validated.

This is the root cause of many project failures.

When a project goes over budget, the consultant has several remedies:

> - Increase the budget
> - Lower the quality
> - Eat the cost
> - Increase the time

That's why the wisest solution is to frontload the project with enough time to gather the information and validate the assumptions, and then, if needed, adjust the budget and schedule.

WHEN YOU GET PAID

In addition to including the estimate of the total cost of the project, you need to define when and how you get paid. I prefer to be paid in advance for each phase of the project. For example, if the project is split up into four phases, one-fourth of the total amount is paid before work begins on the next phase.

This reduces the risk for the client since they are only on the hook for a part of the cost at one time. This also reduces the risk for the consultant, who is paid in advance for the work to be completed.

In my experience, it is far easier to convince the client to pay a fraction of the total project cost up front than it is an attempt to get the entire project paid in advance.

Some projects are done on a time and materials basis. In this case, hours are billed as they are performed.

In the payment section of the SOW, be sure to specify how you want to receive the money: check, money order, wire transfer, or whatever.

Also, include the address of where you want the payment to be sent, as well as who you want the check or money order made out to.

DEFINE THE PROJECT

For a small project, such as creating a graphic image, book cover, or filling in a spreadsheet, a single phase is generally all that you need to define.

On the other hand, many projects tend to be a bit larger in scale. You have two choices in these cases:

> Break the project into smaller subprojects and create an SOW for each one
> split the project up into multiple phases

Statement of work

If I were contracted to write an entire accounting system, for example, I would take the first approach of breaking the project into smaller subprojects. Each application within the accounting system could be a subproject.

This works best when a project can be split into multiple pieces that are more or less independent of one another. They may all have to work together at the end, but they can be analyzed, designed, written, and tested independently.

On the other hand, if I were contracted to ghostwrite a book, write a single application, or build out a computer room, I would tend to take a phased approach, which means one big project that is split into multiple parts.

Generally, the first part is defined as the analysis phase and is used to find out the facts, validate the assumptions, and re-estimate the rest of project. The remaining phases are used to complete the project itself.

This works best when the tasks must be completed one after the other. So the task of phase 1, the analysis and re-estimate, must be completed before beginning phase 2. Phase 2, creating an outline, must be completed before Phase 3. The final phase, writing the document, depends upon the previous phase being successfully completed.

Include a bullet point list on each phase of all of the deliverables for that phase. This is very critical. Focus on deliverables, not how, why, or who. Focus on what you are going to get done.

Just to reiterate, do not get into the how, the why, or the who. That is not important in the SOW, and in fact, can actually be detrimental. Putting the names of people who will do the work brings personalities into scope, and that has no business being in an SOW. As a consultant, you need to ensure you have the freedom to assign people and resources as you see fit. In some cases, you might do the work yourself. Occasionally other resources may fit better. Sometimes, you may even want to outsource parts of the project. Don't allow yourself to be put into the straitjacket that happens when personnel are included in the SOW, unless the client gives you no choice.

DEFINE TERMINATION

I know it seems weird to discuss termination before the project actually begins but is absolutely vital to include that in your SOW.

Ideally, the SOW should state that either party can terminate the contract at any time for any reason. Sometimes it might be necessary to give some amount of notice; this is more important on ongoing service agreements such as monitoring computer systems than it is for creating an application or writing a book.

You also need to specify whether or not any money that is already been paid must be refunded upon contract termination. Generally, it is a good idea to state that money will not be refunded. This is especially true for a small or single-person consulting company.

Statement of work

At the very least, your SOW should state that money paid for services already rendered will not be refunded. You do this by specifying that the money will be prorated. For example, if you created a 12-month project to monitor computer systems and then decided to cancel the project on month five, you should expect to have to refund the amounts for months six through 12. This is because you never delivered any services for those months. However, since you did deliver services for the first five months, that should not be refunded.

You need to be fair in this section. While writing it, put yourself in your client's shoes look at it from their viewpoint as well as your own.

Controlling change

In my experience, one of the largest factors in determining whether a project succeeds or fails is how well change is controlled. This is one of the most sensitive areas of managing and consulting, and also the biggest landmine waiting to blow up in your face if you're not careful.

I'm defining success with these three factors:

- ➢ Completed and delivered
- ➢ Within budget and on time
- ➢ The client is willing to write a testimonial and give good references

Virtually every project will change between signing the SOW and the final delivery. If you don't plan for that change, you are inviting disaster.

When change is managed properly, your client is happy even if the budget is exceeded and the project is delivered late. On the other hand, if change is unmanaged, your client may not be happy even if the budget and schedule are met. Worse yet, you might find yourself taking a loss on the project.

When I was a young manager, back in 1984, I was asked to step in and manage a four-year-old project. It was over two years late, almost 400% over budget and the client held a 10% retainer that would not be delivered until they were satisfied with the product.

Controlling change

The project was quoted as fixed-price, and the SOW was extraordinarily poorly written. The SOW consisted of a single page that basically said we will deliver you a set of applications that allows you to manage your water billing system. No specification was ever written and the analysis was done in parallel with the coding.

As I overviewed the project, I felt like I was in a disaster movie.

In this project, it was impossible to manage change because there was no conclusive definition of what was to be delivered. Without understanding the final product, how can you measure change?

Later in my career, I contracted with a consulting firm to move our computer room from one location to another in a totally different city. This was a difficult project but it went very smoothly, and was completed precisely on time and exactly on budget.

The procedure for handling change was defined in the SOW. As new information came to light, we had a process in place to assess and implement deviations from what we had originally planned.

Whatever the change was needed, the necessary staff from the consulting firm and I got together, discussed what was necessary, and determine how to proceed. We also made a judgment as to whether the schedule needed to change and if additional funding was needed.

Because of this procedure, change became part of our normal process. Without change control, deviations become upsetting, threatening, costly, and confrontational. On the other hand, with the process in place, alterations are handled just by following the procedure.

In other words, plan changes into your project.

The SOW needs to include a statement about how change is managed. At the very least, change needs to be recorded in a log, discussed between the consultant and the client, and agreement on how to proceed needs to occur.

Part of the process is to evaluate if the change results in adjustments to the schedule or the price of the project.

In general, the consulting company should not "eat" the cost of any significant change. Instead, assign a price in both dollars and time to the modification. Some changes do not require an adjustment in either time or dollars; these minor adjustments are still logged and still must be approved by the client.

Sometimes a change will require an adjustment in dollars and time. Discuss these estimates, and get their approval in writing to make the modification to the SOW.

The client's job is to decide if the change is worth the cost. Occasionally, the decision will be made that the change is not necessary or that a different or smaller adjustment can be made for less cost. Quite often, the client will agree to the change for the additional time and money.

You will come across occasions where it's not clear if the change is actually a change. This could happen if the SOW

Controlling change

were incomplete, ambiguous or missing information entirely. In this case, clients will become very insistent that the consulting firm include the "change" within the budget and time originally proposed.

At this point, you as a consultant will need to use your best judgment to determine who pays for the change. In many cases, the only solution is to "split it down the middle," meaning the consultant pays 50% and the client pays 50%.

This is one of the more dangerous parts of any consulting project, and it needs to be handled with extreme care. Be totally honest with your client, and be fair and open-minded about where the responsibility for the change lies.

Clients can become very emotional and protective if they feel that a so-called change is actually part of the original SOW. You may find it's in your best interest to "eat the cost." Just be sure to keep your own emotions out of the discussion, and do the right thing.

Controlling chaos

As a general rule, the amount of chaos that occurs in your project is directly related to how well you manage it. Even if you are working solo, you are still managing yourself as well as the client. You may also be managing people on your own team, people on the client's team, and external consultants.

Sometimes, you're even managing people you wouldn't normally expect to be dealing with. I've often found myself managing the manager of my client, and in a few cases, even the CEO of their company.

You begin managing the project with good communication with your client. Maintain honest and frequent (although not too frequent) meetings, emails, and phone calls to keep things on the right track.

Honesty and integrity are critical to the success of any consulting project. Remain honest with your client and everybody else involved at all times. Sometimes, of course, confidentiality agreements mean you can't say everything to everyone. Outside of that, the moment you decide you need to hide something that you did or that happened, or that you need to lie, is the moment you've started on the road to losing the project and probably the client.

I know that sometimes telling the truth and being honest can be painful, but honesty and integrity are essential parts of your reputation. When referring you to other people, your client will be sure to let them know whether or not you could be trusted.

Controlling chaos

Follow the chain of command in your client's organization. Do not bypass your contact, even if that seems to be the best way to get something done. The only exception to this is if you discover your client is doing something illegal or highly unethical.

Not using the proper chain of command can cause chaos and doom a project to failure.

CLIENT DOES NOT WANT TO BE INVOLVED

Sometimes you run into a situation where the client simply doesn't want to be involved in your project. I've seen this on several occasions.

For example, we were contracted to convert a graphics package from one type of computer to another. Our client delivered the computer containing the software to our office. After that, it was virtually impossible to get anything from them. They had the attitude that they had given us what we needed, and our job was to get it done without their help.

That project was an utter failure. It was difficult to get the simplest question answered, to confirm assumptions, and to get help testing the final product. In hindsight, it was doomed from the start.

The way to combat this tendency is to discuss the need for constant communication with your client before the SOW is even written. Your SOW should include how often meetings will occur, the schedule for status reports, and any other kinds of communications required during the project. During your discussions with your client, ensure you mention the need for regular communication between the two of you.

If you don't have regular and defined communication between you and your client as the project proceeds, you may find that problems don't get solved, decisions are not made, and the project drifts aimlessly.

Prevent this by ensuring your client understands and agrees to the need for communication up front.

THE MICROMANAGING CLIENT

Your client has hired you to get a task completed. Unless you are operating as a temporary employee, you should manage the project yourself. That's part of the job being a consultant.

The SOW includes all of the project deliverables and schedules, possibly modified at the end of phase one or after a pilot project. Because of this, you know what you need to do, when it needs to be completed, and how much you are going to get paid.

You shouldn't need your client to help you with any of this. One of the reasons why you were hired as a consultant is to remove the burden not only of doing the work but of managing the effort from the client.

Be on guard for the client, or one of their staff, who reaches into your project to manage you and the work you are doing. This can be a very touchy situation; some clients are so used to micromanaging that they don't even notice that they are doing it. Some are not comfortable unless they can constantly manage every little thing themselves.

Controlling chaos

This is handled with a well-written SOW, good communication before the project begins, and an honest discussion if it happens.

If you find that your client is micromanaging your efforts, you need to have a discussion with them as soon as possible. A good place to start is to ask them if there's something they are trying to fix. Are schedules not being met? Are the deliverables not being delivered? Are they not getting the communications that they need?

In other words, are they not receiving something that they expect, or, alternately, are they getting something that they don't want.

Don't approach this in a confrontational manner. Your client may be very emotional or touchy on the subject. Ask questions, discuss management styles, and remain levelheaded and honest.

One technique that I've used, which requires a bit of courage, is to point out to the client that a team cannot have two leaders. In one case, I had facts showing that schedules had slipped because of confusion caused by the client trying to manage my own people directly.

Sometimes the micromanaging client can be tolerated because the effects are not great. If the project is put in jeopardy, you can always exercise the termination clause that you built into your SOW. Don't bluff if you do this. It's possible your client will get the message and back off. If he doesn't, carry through and terminate the project.

Meetings

The biggest time waster on any project, consulting or otherwise, is an unmanaged meeting. Think about a meeting for a moment. Let's say, for example, you have called six other people together in the conference room for an hour to discuss project status.

One of those people arrives 10 minutes late. Your typical manager will delay the start of the meeting by 10 minutes. This wasted 10 minutes of time for everybody who was on time.

Once the meeting gets started, another five or 10 minutes is wasted getting everybody on the same page, overviewing what happened last time, or dealing with small talk.

If there is no agenda, which is pretty normal for most meetings, then you have no guarantee that everything that needs to be discussed gets talked about, and decisions that are required may not get made.

Quite often, people will bring their cell phones, laptops, tablets, and other electronic devices to the meeting. Inevitably, someone's phone will ring and they will have to leave the room to take a call.

Even worse, some of the people at the meeting won't even be listening. They'll be busy doing something that more or less resembles work on the laptop or tablet they brought to the meeting, or they might be texting on their phone.

Meetings

As you can see, an unmanaged meeting is not only worthless but may actually be counterproductive. The time is wasted, and it's sheer luck whether anything valuable gets done.

On the other hand, a well-managed meeting is a joy to virtually everyone in attendance. Only those people who need to be there are invited, and each of them receives an agenda in advance with enough time to read it and understand its contents.

Make it a firm rule that when the meeting starts, all external communication stops. You might even ask everyone to leave their cell phones on a shelf outside the door.

You have to handle the instance of someone texting or playing around on the laptop during the meeting with utter brutality. If they work for you, you make them stop; if they don't, you politely ask them to pay attention.

As a general rule, meetings need to be less than an hour long. My habit is to schedule a meeting for 50 minutes to leave time for people to get somewhere else at the top of the hour. I have found through hard experience that, with few exceptions, a meeting that lasts longer than an hour is a complete waste of time.

The same holds true for interviews. When you're interviewing someone, plan on spending less than an hour unless you have no choice. This is respectful of their time, and I found that the interview sputters out at about the hour point anyway. If you must schedule interviews that last a long time, break them up with short 15 minute breaks every hour. Longer interviews might be necessary if you have someone coming in from out of town or a person with limited availability.

Through long and hard experience, I found that having meetings over lunch or dinner is not only worthless but counterproductive. People tend to focus on eating and not listening or talking. Avoid scheduling meetings over lunch or dinner, except in the case of an emergency.

If you have the option, include a few glasses and some water in any meeting is going to last longer than 45 minutes. Make sure it is water and not soda or juice. The sugar tends to put people to sleep.

Meetings should always start on time. Don't ever delay starting a meeting because someone is late. Obviously, there are some exceptions to this rule. If I was having a meeting with the CEO of a major company and he or she was late, I'd certainly wait. But in general, start the meeting on time and don't wait for people. If you wait, you are rewarding their unethical behavior.

And yes, being late to a meeting without a good reason (sometimes there are valid reasons to be late) is unethical and unprofessional behavior. Handle it as such and it will stop. If you treat it lightly, then the behavior will continue, and you have no right to be upset about it.

I've used some techniques to handle latecomers. Depending on the situation, I may be gentle, or I might go with the sledgehammer approach.

Meetings

A simple method is just to lock the door soon as the meeting starts and not allow any latecomers to attend. That only works if people actually want to attend the meeting.

I've had occasions where I wrote people up for being late to or missing meetings. This went on their permanent personnel record, but it tends to have a somewhat demoralizing effect.

One successful tactic that I've used on occasion is that anyone who was late had to stand through the whole meeting. That seems to work well for the most part.

All meetings need an agenda, which is a list of what is to be accomplished during the meeting. You could think of it as the deliverables from the group. If your meeting doesn't have an agenda, you're almost certainly wasting everyone's time.

As a general rule, the agenda should be sent to all attendees at least one day before the meeting. This gives everyone a chance to get their facts together and think about what's going to be discussed.

In the case of an emergency, meetings are called abruptly. In this instance, the first and only item initially on the agenda is to complete the agenda. This lets everyone know why they are in the room.

We had a major computer outage that affected the entire company. I called a meeting of almost 40 people to get everyone on the same page about the disaster and what we needed to do. I began the meeting with a brief summary of why everybody was there and then created the agenda on the spot. It was an extraordinarily productive meeting even though all those 40 people had less than 15 minutes of notice to be there. This was because, within the first five minutes of the meeting, they knew why they were there and what we intended to do.

Making an agenda is a simple exercise. Create a document, and use bullet points to list everything that needs to be done at the meeting. Don't list why, how, or who; focus on what needs to be accomplished.

If you expect a decision to be made, treat that as something that needs to be done. For example, record "Make a decision about the start date of the project," as a bullet point on your agenda.

Include topics needed to be discussed in bullet points. Your bullet point might be "Discuss the design of the application and decide on the inputs." Everyone at the meeting understands there's going to be a discussion, and better still they know what the discussion is intended to do.

As you work through the agenda, keep a record of what was accomplished. Include what decisions were made, who made them, and any other information you need to note. As soon as practical after the meeting, write up the minutes and send them out to everyone who attended.

You don't need to write a long dissertation on everything that happened in the meeting. Take each bullet point on your agenda, and note as sub-bullet points (indent them one deeper) whatever needs to be noted about that agenda item. Keep it brief and focus on decisions made and things that were done.

Meetings

The minutes should be sent out the same day as the meeting occurred if at all possible. If you take good notes during the meeting, the minutes should only take a short time to prepare; anywhere from 5 to 15 minutes should be enough. If you are spending more than that a lot of time, you are writing too much in your minutes.

Communicating with the client

Frequent and accurate communication with the right people at the appropriate times is the key to the success of your project. Any problem, any issue, any overrun, or anything else that happens can be handled with good and honest communication.

Some of the reasons a project will become rough or fail include:

> - Not acknowledging emails
> - Not answering emails promptly
> - Being afraid to call your client when there's a problem or emergency
> - Failing to send your client regular status reports
> - Failing to have regular meetings when needed in person, or via Skype or telephone conference call

On the other hand, if you want to have a successful project, lay the groundwork with good communication skills. Some of the things you can do include:

> - Acknowledge every email promptly
> - When your client emails you with a question, answer it promptly and thoroughly
> - If there is a problem get in touch with the client right away
> - Send out regular status reports, so your client knows what is going on
> - Schedule regular meetings, if appropriate, by phone, by Skype, or in person

Communicating with the client

There are several ways you can communicate with your client, and these are summarized below:

➢ **In person:** this is the best method for performing interviews, presales meetings, and delivering something.

➢ **Email:** take advantage of email for routine communications and for summarizing what was discussed during phone calls and meetings. Email is the ideal form of communication most of the time, as it is nonintrusive, remains in your clients inbox until it can be read, and can be kept as a permanent record.

➢ **Phone call:** use the phone for urgent communications or when time is important. Always follow-up phone calls with an email summarizing what was discussed. Consider recording all phone calls, but be sure you let everyone on the call know that is being recorded.

➢ **Skype or similar application:** video chat applications such as Skype are useful substitutes for in-person meetings on occasion. Any call or meeting via Skype or similar application should be recorded, and you should let everyone involved know that it is being recorded.

➢ **Text messages:** make it a rule never to use text messaging to communicate with your clients, staff, and consultants. Text messaging is not generally a valid form of communication for professionals to use.

PHONE CALLS

The phone is a perfectly valid way to communicate with your client. If you have something that is urgent, make a call. I've had team members who were very reluctant to use the phone to talk to clients, and this often led to problems.

This is because, outside of a phone call, there is no automatic acknowledgment. In other words, unless your client replies, you can't confirm that they actually received your message. For all you know, they could be out of town, on vacation, may have been fired, or their email server may be down.

Always follow up any phone communication with an email that summarizes the conversation. Don't spend a lot of time writing this email. Quickly summarize what was discussed and any decisions that were made. Be professional, thorough, and make sure your spelling and grammar are correct.

Before picking up the phone and calling your client, acknowledge that phones are very intrusive. Most people carry a smartphone with them and answer it when it rings. If your client is in a meeting or lunch, you're likely to interrupt them. If your message is not urgent, email might be a better way to communicate it.

FREQUENCY OF COMMUNICATION

Communicating with your client too often can also be a problem. Sometimes it's tempting to send an email for every stray thought that comes into your mind.

The schedule for normal, everyday communications should be spelled out in your SOW. These include status reports and

Communicating with the client

how often they are done, interviews and meetings, and other nonemergency messages.

For most projects, I write a short weekly status report that includes what was done during the previous week. Any time there's a phone call, I send a report of what was discussed. If meetings or interviews are scheduled, the agenda is sent out in advance and minutes are sent out afterward.

Of course, acknowledge and respond to any emails from the client or a subcontractor quickly.

If you sent an email and your client hasn't responded, wait a decent amount of time before sending another email. People do have other things to do. I will usually wait at least a few hours, and sometimes even until the next day before sending a follow-up message.

This isn't something you should be overly concerned about, nor should you spend any time fretting about the number of emails you're sending. Keep in mind that your client is hiring you to offload work. You were hired because you are skilled, and sending too many emails or messages tends to make it appear like you can't manage your project.

Of course, if the situation is urgent or an emergency, you should be sending emails, picking up the phone, or having face-to-face meetings as often as needed.

TEXT MESSAGING

Text messaging should never be used for communicating with your client. Let me stress that: do not use text messages—

including instant messaging—to communicate with your client.

Possibly second only to using homing pigeons, texting is the worst possible method to communicate anything of any significance to anyone.

Communication via text message has the following problems:

> ➢ There is no acknowledgment that the text message was received.
> ➢ People often don't check their text messages on a regular basis, so if they don't get it immediately, it may sit there for a long period of time before being read.
> ➢ Some people don't like typing on the small keywords on their smartphone.
> ➢ It is difficult, if not impossible, to keep a permanent record of text communications.
> ➢ Text messages can be very intrusive to meetings and conversations.

Using text messaging to communicate anything of any significance to your client is unprofessional behavior.

If you do communicate via text, keep the messages short, and follow up with an email summarizing the discussion.

EMAILS

Acknowledge all email messages promptly. It only takes a few seconds. Hit the reply button (make sure it's not reply all) type "Thank you," "I understand," or a similar message. Press the send key.

Communicating with the client

You may not have time at that moment to actually address the question or concern of the client. In that case, reply with a message like, "Thank you, I'll review your message this afternoon and get back to you by tomorrow morning." This tells your client that you got his message and value his concern. It also lets them know when you'll get back to them.

Professionals acknowledge emails promptly and efficiently. This way your client at least knows that you received the message. One of the signs of being unprofessional is a failure to acknowledge email messages promptly.

Any time an email message requires a reply, send one as soon as you can. This is different than an acknowledgment. A reply answers the question or addresses the concern.

TYPES OF REPORTING

Communicate any problems or concerns about the project with your client promptly and efficiently. Sometimes it is important not to communicate too quickly; you might have to take some time to gather information before you contact them.

All but the smallest projects deserve regular status reports. Status reports can simply be an email message sent out on a regular basis; the frequency should be included in your SOW.

The purpose of the status report is to let your client know how your project is doing at that moment in time. Emergencies need to be communicated immediately; status reports are used for routine communications.

A status report should be brief. In general, you should be able to read the entire thing without scrolling the screen. You should be able to write one within 10 to 15 minutes at the most. If you're spending longer than that writing a status report, you are including too much information.

Don't include fancy graphs that show the percentage complete of each phase of the project. Don't attach Gantt charts, spreadsheets, and other detailed data as part of your status report. These take up valuable time that could be better used actually getting things done. Sometimes, however, clients insist on more detailed status reports; in these cases, make sure that's included in your SOW, factored into your project schedules, and you've added the cost of the project to account for the time. The time spent to write status reports is not free; often you can handle a client who wants overly detailed reporting by gently pointing out that fact.

Do include any agreed-upon statistics that measure your progress. For example, in a project to write a book, one of the statistics might be the number of words completed per week. Include that in your status report. Just keep it simple and make sure the statistics are specified in your SOW.

A frequent mistake made by many consultants is to use status reports as a method of "covering their butt." That is not the purpose of the status report; instead, you should be communicating to your client an honest appraisal of the progress made the last time status was reported. If there is a need to "cover your butt," that should be done as a separate email or letter.

Make the focus of your status report covering what has been completed since the last status report, and any exceptions

Communicating with the client

that have occurred. There is no need to discuss tasks that are in progress. Focus on what was finished and what was planned that didn't happen.

Your SOW and possibly a more detailed project plan specifies when tasks are supposed to be completed. You should make it a rule on your status report to discuss the exceptions, such as tests that are late. You might say, for example, "All tasks on time as per schedule, excluding…" or something similar.

Do not send status reports as an attachment to email messages. It's quite common for people to miss an attachment and never read it all. Your status should be in the body of the email message.

The primary reason why you keep status reports short is so your client reads them. Anything longer than a few paragraphs, a dozen at the most, will not be read by virtually everyone on the project or by your client.

Most people will scan through the first half-dozen or dozen paragraphs and then stop reading. Structure your status report appropriately by including the important information of the top nonetheless critical information at the bottom.

Reading status reports should be optional. A status report is simply that: a report on the current state of the project. It should not be used to communicate assignments, orders, or discussions. The only purpose of them is to say, "This is where we stand as of today."

In summary, keep your communications frequent, but not too frequent, as well as brief and to the point. Control your meetings and keep them short and on topic.

Record everything

I make it a point to record any phone calls made between my clients and me, and to record all meetings that occur. This is in addition to normal note taking and minutes.

These recordings are especially useful when doing interviews. It can be difficult to take precise notes of what is said while interviewing, and it is very useful to be able to review the exact words at will.

Permission indicating that recording is okay with them must be received from all parties. I make it a point to do this at the beginning of the conversation so the approval is part of the recording. To date, no client has ever objected to recording a conversation.

Recordings become part of the project archives, and the date and time are included in the filename, along with a brief description of the conversation. This makes it relatively easy to find at a later date. The minutes and agenda of the meeting, if applicable, are filed in the same place, as are any notes or other documents from the meeting.

As a general rule, these recordings should not be sent to your client. They are for your own reference if you need to reconstruct what was said during the meeting. I would also not recommend transcribing these recordings. It's generally not worth the trouble.

I found these recordings to be valuable. Primarily, merely having the recording available seems to reduce or eliminate

Record everything

discussions about what was said or disagreements about commitments and such.

There are several applications available on any smartphone that allow phone calls to be recorded. These generally cost only a few dollars. They are very simple to use because most of them have a setting to allow the recording to start as soon as the connection is made.

I prefer making calls from my computer because I can use an application such as Skype. Plug-ins are available for Skype that will automatically record both audio only or video plus audio communications.

For meetings, I use a Google Chromebook with an application called Mic Note. This handy tool records what is said in the meeting and allows notes to be taken at the same time. A timestamp is created for each line in the notes that corresponds directly to a time in the recording. This makes it very simple to find specific points in the recording later.

Anything written on a whiteboard, post-it notes on the wall, blackboards, and so forth should be photographed and filed along with the agenda and notes.

Any kind of knowledge transfer or training sessions should be videoed if at all possible. This allows that knowledge to be directly communicated to other project members at will.

Just make sure you get the permission of everyone involved to make the recording, and ensure that permission is recorded at the start of the conversation. Alternately, you can include permission to record as part of your SOW. By signing that document, your client explicitly gives you permission to record.

Outsourcing

Some consultants fail more often than they should because they think they need to do all the work themselves. There is an erroneous belief that it's cheaper to do the work internally than to ship it outside.

I've run into consultants that believe subcontracting is somehow immoral or unethical. Others have felt the client will think less of them because they subcontract.

Actually, subcontracting can be an excellent way to expand the services you can offer and improve the speed and quality of your work.

For example, if you were contracted to write an application, you could easily justify hiring a subcontractor for a brief time to ensure the product used proper security. At one company where I worked, we had a security audit every year. We hired a security company to do that audit, and they often hired a consultant to do specialized tasks such as penetration testing.

I have successfully used subcontractors in my consulting projects many times. As a ghostwriter, which is basically a writer consulting to create a book, I hire cover artists, keyword analyzers, and proofreaders. In the computer field, I would hire people with specialized talents when it didn't make sense to have a full-time staff member do those things. For example, I usually hired a consultant to do the technical writing or to create the user manuals for the project.

Outsourcing

Don't be afraid to use subcontractors. It doesn't matter if you're a one-man shop or if you have hundreds of employees on staff; subcontracting work out can save you money and expand the services you offer to your clients.

If you're a single person or very small consulting company, the creative use of subcontractors means you don't have to learn everything about everything. You can bid on jobs knowing that you can find people to do the task and your mission changes to managing those subcontractors.

As consulting companies get larger, they sometimes get the idea that they need to do everything in-house. Managers often have a "gut feeling" that contractors are more expensive than in-house staff. In actuality, this is completely false.

By hiring subcontractors to do specific tasks, you are not hiring permanent staff. This reduces your costs, as you don't pay benefits or taxes to consultants. You also reduce your training costs because you don't need to train in-house staff on every possible technology.

The issue with subcontractors is the same issue you have when you hire people. The quality can vary greatly from person to person. Sometimes you'll find a subcontractor who is worth his or her weight in gold; other times they cause more harm than good.

When you find a good subcontractor, hang onto them. Keep the contact information in your address book and send work to them from time to time. Conversely, don't send work to subcontractors who are subpar; it's wrong to encourage substandard work.

When you're consulting, don't be afraid to use subcontractors from time to time. It will make your job much easier, and you'll be able to offer more to your clients.

Things to avoid

Sometimes you find yourself working very closely with the client. Occasionally your client is a friend or relative. Regardless of the relationship, treat them the same as every other client.

As a consultant, it's important to know the difference between a "good" client and a "bad" client.

Good clients pay on time, don't try to nickel and dime you, follow the procedures and guidelines stipulated in your SOW, and don't make constant attempts to get you to work for free. These are the clients that are a joy to work with.

Then there are those that I call bad clients. A bad client wants you to work for free and often attempts to finagle lower rates and extra unpaid hours. Also, they have difficulty understanding the purpose of the SOW and make constant attempts to get changes that are out of scope added to the project without additional cost. And, of course, bad clients don't pay on time and occasionally don't pay at all.

It's important in your role as a consultant to encourage good client behavior and discourage bad client behavior.

There are two ways you can be paid as a consultant. You can be paid in a phased approach; in this method you get paid in advance for a portion of the project at a time. In the second approach, you bill for hours worked and you get paid for them; in this method you typically paid after the work is done.

Things to avoid

As a consultant, my ironclad rule is a late or missed payment means the work stops. It is completely unacceptable for a client to be late with a payment, to not pay the full amount due, or to not pay at all. If your money doesn't come in on time, stop working and call the client immediately. No matter what the client says, don't start working again until you receive payment. Be nice but be firm.

Talk to the client about why the payment is late and work out any differences of opinion that may have led to the situation. If the client is withholding payment for some real or imagined slight, discuss it and if it's valid and get it fixed.

Regardless of the reason, withholding or shorting payment is serious. If a client has a grievance, it is far better for them to communicate with you, and if necessary, terminate the contract. Withholding payment is not an acceptable solution.

And you, as a consultant, should not tolerate it. Generally, I found that when payment has been withheld, is late, or is not complete, it's the handwriting on the wall that the end is near. As long as your SOW allows you to terminate the contract, then consider that option.

Your SOW should spell out the procedures, in general, by which your project operates, as well as other things like deliverables and the scope of the work. Your client agreed to those procedures by signing the SOW. Changes can be made later after appropriate discussions, but it's important not to allow changes to be made willy-nilly or at will.

For example, early in my career we contracted with a client to develop and code an accounting system. The SOW was actually fairly well done. The client kept adding new functions and new applications to the system, and for various reasons we allowed them to do so. Because of that, we actually wound up losing money on the project.

Don't allow changes in scope or your procedures to occur without following your change control procedures. If your SOW states that you will do an interview once per week with your client (as when you're writing a book, for example) and the client finds he can't do one per week, then create a change request and get the client to agree to it.

Otherwise, you may find yourself being blamed by the client for the project running late when the client wasn't following the terms of the agreement. But since you didn't document that, it may be difficult to prove.

Good clients understand this concept and are happy to follow the procedures that they agreed upon. They are also happy to follow your change control process.

During the pre-sales and sales processes, when you're trying to convince your client to do business with you, you can expect some negotiations. This is a normal part of doing business as a consultant. However, keep your eyes and ears open for warning signs during the negotiation process.

For example, we had one client with whom we spent six months meeting over and over again to convince them to fund the project. We must have put in dozens of hours of presales work. This was a project that should've cost around $10,000. By the time we were awarded the contract, it was for $3,000.

Things to avoid

While it is true that sometimes clients do need to go back, get approvals, and work with budgets, it's generally a bad sign when the presales process goes on for much longer than it should.

First of all, those dozens of hours that were spent trying to get this client to sign a contract could have been better spent actually working on contracts we had signed or pursuing work that was easier to close.

Second, the client turned out to have money issues and we wound up having to spend a couple of dozen more hours trying to collect the money that was owed us.

Pay attention to what happens during the negotiation process. Look for signs that the client may not pay, doesn't have the money, doesn't have approval, tries to nickel and dime a contract, and so forth.

Here's an example of a negotiation that went well: I sat down with a client recently and said I thought the project was about $20,000. We negotiated the price down to $15,000. It was a quick and simple negotiation that took about 15 minutes. After that, I delivered the SOW. It was signed within a few days. It was quick, easy and didn't feel like a tug-of-war.

Good clients are worth their weight in gold, and those are the ones you should encourage by allowing them to do business with you and by, if necessary, giving special rates or whatever another incentive you want to give.

Bad clients, on the other hand, will drag you down, lose you money, and frustrate any subcontractors or employees you have working for you. They are stressful and are not worth the effort. Don't encourage them by giving them incentives, allowing them to do business with you (at least a second time), or giving them special rates.

Bad clients simply aren't worth the trouble.

THE CLIENT IS NOT YOUR FRIEND

Regardless of whether your client is your friend or family member, when involved in a project, you must treat them as a client. In other words, these are people that you have a business arrangement with, and they should be dealt with accordingly.

Negotiate with everybody the same. It is best not to give special favors to friends or family members as far as rates are concerned.

Manage the project the same way, regardless of the relationship of the parties involved.

Supervise any people involved in the project identically whether they are complete strangers or best friends.

Be nice about it. There is no need to be rude or abrasive. Just treat everybody the same.

This eliminates the possibility of being accused of favoritism and of being taken advantage of due to a relationship.

Sometimes friends or family will ask for, or demand, special handling. This is especially true of payment. Friends may ask for special rates that you wouldn't give anyone else. Family

Things to avoid

members may ask you to relax penalties. My advice is to treat them the same as everyone else.

WORK FOR FREE

It is very important to be aware of the scope of your project. This is defined by your SOW and possibly, for larger projects, various types of specifications.

If changes are requested or become necessary, they must be recorded and understood. You have to evaluate every change to determine if it will result in an additional cost of money or time.

Never assume that you'll do a change at no cost. Always take the time to review the change and analyze its impact on the schedule and cost. Once you have that information, you can make a decision as to whether you're going to absorb it yourself or pass it on to your client.

In all cases, the client should be made aware of the change and its impact on the project. For no cost changes, you can do this as line items on your regular status report.

If the change results in additional fees or a schedule change, you must get approval from your client. It is generally best to get these approvals in writing, and if possible, signed by the client.

The mechanism for controlling change needs to be defined as part of your SOW.

When it goes south

Every once in a while, in spite of your best efforts, a project will go south. It's running late, it's over budget, changes are happening at an incredible rate, the staff is turning over quickly, and the client is very unhappy.

This happens when a project is not managed well. Virtually everything can be controlled by a good project manager. If the project is not proceeding according to plan, that's a sign that it's not being controlled.

One major cause of the project spiraling out of control is multiple people acting as managers. This causes the team members assigned to project to receive contradicting orders from different people in authority. If this is happening, you, as the official project manager, need to bring it to a stop immediately. Find out where the cross orders are coming from and handle it. If you can't get the person to stop, no matter what you try, then consider terminating the project. **It is virtually impossible for a project of any significant size to succeed where there is more than one person acting as manager**.

Another cause of failure is uncontrolled change. Follow the process you've outlined in your SOW for handling change control. Investigate and find out when it hasn't been followed and correct it. **If change is not well controlled on a project, then it's highly likely the project will not succeed**.

Sometimes the problem is a bad apple. This is the person who pretends he's part of the project but is actually working behind the scenes to sabotage everything. If you suspect this, watch how people act in meetings, take a look at their communications, read their emails (if allowed legally and within your company), and see if you can overhear some conversations among teammates.

If you find someone is working to sabotage the project (or is just incompetent), then you either need to handle them or fire them from the project. Do not tolerate any bad apples on your team. Of course, this can be more difficult if this person is on your client's team. In that case, you may need to have a conversation with your client.

I've run into projects that failed because the client didn't want them to succeed. This is pretty rare, but it does happen. I've had a client who was forced by his manager to do a project that he didn't agree with. At every opportunity, he tried to sabotage our work. This is a very difficult situation to deal with, and it may require a private and off the record conversation with your client.

Sadly, one cause of project failure that I've run across the few times the substance abuse. Early in my career, I hired a technical writer who had a drinking problem that affected her work. This led to some very awkward conversations until she was finally terminated.

Once in a while, especially in larger projects, you may find that you severely underestimated the amount of effort (money or time) required to get it done. The best handling here is to gather up your facts and have a conversation with your client. You have the option of asking for more money, splitting the cost down the middle, eating the cost yourself, or exiting the project using the termination clause (assuming you at one end of the SOW.)\

Another thing that can cause a project to go south is if your client doesn't have the time to deal with it. You were hired to free up time for your client, but that doesn't mean that you should be ignored or that the client has no responsibilities at all. In this case, you need to have a discussion with the client and together come up with a resolution. I've had cases where this caused the project to be put on hold. Another was canceled, and another where the client just told to do the best we could. This is always very awkward and difficult to handle. Just talk to the client and see if you can come up with a resolution.

The best way to keep your project from going south is to manage it tightly at all times. Don't micromanage your people, as that tends to reduce productivity. Just stay on top of things, communicate well with your client, and do your job as a project manager.

The end of the project

Well, you finally did it. Congratulations! The project is finished.

How do you know when it's done? That should be clearly identified in your SOW, and if it's not, you might have a problem.

Usually, completion is not just delivering a product. Sometimes the product will need to be reviewed and accepted by the client. This can produce extra work if the client doesn't agree.

The way to prevent unforeseen extra costs at the end of a project is to build in reviews by the client at periodic points through the project. This is very easy if you split the project up into phases or subprojects. Each of them is treated as a separate entity with its own deliverables. When the whole project is finally delivered, all of its parts have already been approved. The only question left is if the pieces work together?

Deliver your final product to the client, get the appropriate sign-offs, and you're done. You must get the client to sign a letter or note indicating that they have accepted the finished product. In the case of freelancer websites, that's included as part of the process.

Depending on the size of the project, I like to schedule a final meeting with my client to formally hand over the deliverables. The method of handover should be specified in your SOW. You might send documents as email attachments or on a USB

The end of the project

key, code might be delivered on a hard drive, or you may hand over the passwords to an administrator account on their website.

Sometimes the client will not agree that you are finished. This requires a conversation, of course, to determine their disagreement. If their points are valid, address them and redeliver the product. If you believe that those changes require additional cost, discuss that with your client and come to an agreement.

Be wary at this point in the project to changes in scope. If you have a good relationship with your client and you've maintained that throughout the project, this generally is not a problem. But if the project has been rough or the client has generally been uncooperative, you may find they attempt to add a few "small things" at the end before they'll sign off on the work.

The best way to handle this is to treat all of those "small things" through your change control system. If they require more money, let your client know. If they don't, then complete them and redeliver the project.

Be careful about agreeing to make changes without going through your change control process. Sometimes it's tempting, since the end is so close, to just give in and do those "few minor things." Do that at your own risk.

Hopefully, you've done enough things right that the project is finished, it's within budget, and on time. Note that the definition of "within budget and on time" may be different from when you started because of changes in scope.

Before you leave the room during that final sign off, ask your client to write a testimonial. If at all possible, get them to write it then and there. The best and easiest time to get a testimonial is at the successful close of a project.

If the client says he doesn't have the time or doesn't want to write it, offer to write it yourself. In fact, it's best to have it ready for them before you go into the meeting for the final signoff. In this case, just give it to them and ask him if they agree with it. When I've done this with a client, they typically make a couple of minor changes (if any at all) and went and accepted what I'd written.

Get that final testimonial. This is vital to getting additional business down the line.

Once you have that in your hand, you are finally done with the project.

Congratulations.

Conclusion

Projects need to be well-managed, regardless of whether they are a five dollar book cover on fiverr.com or a multimillion dollar effort with 20 different team members.

Obviously, the amount of effort to manage a small project is different than the amount needed to manage a humongous one. The key point is to communicate with your client, ensure you have a good statement of work (or the equivalent), and that you actually perform project management.

This book summarizes a few of the concepts that I've learned in my 35-year career. About a third of that career was spent working as a vice president of consulting for two different firms. The rest of it I spent hiring consultants to do work that needed to be done.

Thus, I have worked both sides of the fence. I understand what it feels like to be a consultant and what a consultant requires for success. I also understand the point of view of the client, and what the client needs to be successful.

I hope what I've written here proves to be beneficial to you as you proceed in your consulting career.

BEFORE YOU GO
If you scroll to the last page in this eBook, you will have the opportunity to leave feedback and share the book with Before You Go. I'd be grateful if you turned to the last page and shared the book.

Conclusion

Also, if you have time, please leave a review. Positive reviews are incredibly useful. If you didn't like the book, please email me at rich@thewritingking.com and I'd be happy to get your input.

linkedin.thewritingking.com

About the Author

https://www.linkedin.com/in/richardlowejr
Feel free to send a connection request

Follow me on Twitter: @richardlowejr

Richard Lowe has leveraged more than 35 years of experience as a Senior Computer Manager and Designer at four companies into that of a bestselling author, blogger, ghostwriter, and public speaker. He has written hundreds of articles for blogs and ghostwritten more than a dozen books and has published manuscripts about computers, the Internet, surviving disasters, management, and human rights. He is currently working on a ten-volume science fiction series – the Peacekeeper Series – to be published at the rate of three volumes per year, beginning in 2016.

Richard started in the field of Information Technology, first as the Vice President of Consulting at Software Techniques, Inc. Because he craved action, after six years he moved on to work for two companies at the same time: he was the Vice President of Consulting at Beck Computer Systems and the Senior Designer at BIF Accutel. In January 1994, Richard found a home at Trader Joe's as the Director of Technical Services and Computer Operations. He remained with that incredible company for almost 20 years before taking an early retirement to begin a new life as a professional writer. He is currently the CEO of The Writing King, a company that provides all forms of writing services, the owner of The EBay King, and a Senior Branding Expert for LinkedIn Makeover. You can find a current list of all books on his Author Page and

About the Author

take a look at his exclusive line of coloring books at <u>The</u> <u>Coloring King</u>.

Richard has a quirky sense of humor and has found that life is full of joy and wonder. As he puts it, "This little ball of rock, mud, and water we call Earth is an incredible place, with many secrets to discover. Beings fill our corner of the universe, and some are happy, and others are sad, but each has their unique story to tell."

His philosophy is to take life with a light heart, and he approaches each day as a new source of happiness. Evil is ignored, discarded, or defeated; good is helped, enriched, and fulfilled. One of his primary interests is to educate people about their human rights and assist them to learn how to be happy in life.

Richard spent many happy days hiking in national parks, crawling over boulders, and peering at Indian pictographs. He toured the Channel Islands off Santa Barbara and stared in fascination at wasps building their homes in Anza-Borrego. One of his joys is photography, and he has photographed more than 1,200 belly dancing events, as well as dozens of Renaissance fairs all over the country.

Because writing is his passion, Richard remains incredibly creative and prolific; each day he writes between 5,000 and 10,000 words, diligently using language to bring life to the world so that others may learn and be entertained.

Richard is the CEO of The Writing King, which specializes in fulfilling any writing need. You can find out more at https://www.thewritingking.com/, and emails are welcome at rich@thewritingking.com

Books by Richard G Lowe Jr.

<u>Business Professional Series</u>

<u>On the Professional Code of Ethics and Business Conduct in the Workplace – Professional Ethics: 100 Tips to Improve Your Professional Life</u> - have you ever wondered what it takes to be successful in the professional world? This book gives you some tips that will improve your job and your career.

<u>Help! My Boss is Whacko! - How to Deal with a Hostile Work Environment</u> - sometimes the problem is the boss. There are all kinds of managers, some competent, some incompetent, and others just plain whacked. This book will help you understand and handle those different types of managers.

<u>Help! I've Lost My Job: Tips on What to do When You're Unexpectedly Unemployed</u> – suddenly having to leave your job can be a harsh and emotional time in your life. Learn some of the things that you need to consider and handle if this happens to you.

<u>Help! My Job Sucks Insider Tips on Making Your Job More Satisfying and Improving Your Career</u> – sometimes conditions conspire to make the regular trek to a job feel like a trip through Dante's Inferno. Sometimes, these are out of our control, such as a malicious manager or incompetent colleague. On the other hand, we can take control of our lives and workplace and improve our situation. Get this book to learn what you can do when your job sucks.

Books by Richard G Lowe Jr.

How to Manage a Consulting Project: Make money, get your project done on time, and get referred again and again – I found that being a consultant is a great way to earn a living. Managing a consulting project can be a challenge. This book contains some tips to help you so you can deliver a better product or service to your customers.

How to be a Good Manager and Supervisor, and How to Delegate – Lessons Learned from the Trenches: Insider Secrets for Managers and Supervisors – I've been a manager for over thirty years I learned many things about how to get the job done and deliver quality service. The information in this book will help you manage your projects to a high level of quality.

Focus on LinkedIn – Learn how to create a LinkedIn profile and to network effectively using the #1 business social media site.

Home Computer Security Series

Safe Computing is Like Safe Sex: You have to practice it to avoid infection – Security expert and Computer Executive, Richard Lowe, presents the simple steps you can take to protect your computer, photos and information from evil doers and viruses. Using easy-to-understand examples and simple explanations, Lowe explains why hackers want your system, what they do with your information, and what you can do to keep them at bay. Lowe answers the question: how to you keep yourself say in the wild west of the internet.

Disaster Preparation and Survival Series

Real World Survival Tips and Survival Guide: Preparing for and Surviving Disasters with Survival Skills – CERT (Civilian Emergency Response Team) trained and Disaster Recovery Specialist, Richard Lowe, lays out how to make you, your family, and your friends ready for any disaster, large or small. Based upon specialized training, interviews with experts and personal experience, Lowe answers the big question: what is the secret to improving the odds of survival even after a big disaster?

Creating a Bug Out Bag to Save Your Life: What you need to pack for emergency evacuations - When you are ordered to evacuate—or leave of your free will—you probably won't have a lot of time to gather your belongings and the things you'll need. You may have just a few minutes to get out of your home. The best preparation for evacuation is to create what is called a bug out bag. These are also known as go-bags, as in, "grab it and go!"

Professional Freelance Writer Series

How to Operate a Freelance Writing Business, and How to be a Ghostwriter – Proven Tips and Tricks Every Author Needs to Know about Freelance Writing: Insider Secrets from a Professional Ghostwriter – This book explains how to be a ghostwriter, and gives tips on everything from finding customers to creating a statement of work to delivering your final product.

How to Write a Blog That Sells and How to Make Money From Blogging: Insider Secrets from a Professional Blogger:

Books by Richard G Lowe Jr.

Proven Tips and Tricks Every Blogger Needs to Know to Make Money – There is an art to writing an article that prompts the reader to make a decision to do something. That's the narrow focus of this book. You will learn how to create an article that gets a reader interested, entices them, informs them, and causes them to make a decision when they reach the end.

<u>Other Books by Richard Lowe Jr</u>

<u>How to Be Friends with Women: How to Surround Yourself with Beautiful Women without Being Sleazy</u> – I am a photographer and frequently find myself surrounded by some of the most beautiful women in the world. This book explains how men can attract women and keep them as friends, which can often lead to real, fulfilling relationships.

<u>How to Throw Parties like a Professional: Tips to Help You Succeed with Putting on a Party Event</u> – Many of us have put on parties, and I know it can be a daunting and confusing experience. In this book, I share what I learned from hosting small house parties to shows and events.

Additional Resources

Is your career important to you? Find out how to move your career in any direction you desire, improve your long-term livelihood, and be prepared for any eventuality. Visit the page below to sign up to receive valuable tips via email, and to get a free eBook about how to optimize your LinkedIn profile.

http://list.thewritingking.com/

I've written and published many books on a variety of subjects. They are all listed on the following page.

https://www.thewritingking.com/books/

On that site, I also publish articles about business, writing, and other subjects. You can visit by clicking the following link:

https://www.thewritingking.com

To find out more about me or my photography, you can visit these sites:

Personal website: https://www.richardlowe.com
Photography: http://www.richardlowejr.com
LinkedIn Profile: https://www.linkedin.com/in/richardlowejr
Twitter: https://twitter.com/richardlowejr

If you have any comments about this book, feel free to email me at rich@thewritingking.com

Premium Writing Services

Do you have a story that needs to be told? Have you been trying to write a book for ages but never can seem to find the time to get it done? Do you want to brand your business, but don't know how to get started?

The Writing King has the answer. We can help you with any of your writing needs.

Ghostwriting. We can write your book, which entails interviewing you to get your story, writing the book and then working with you to revise it until complete. To discuss your book, contact The Writing King today.

Website Copy. Many businesses include the text on their sites as an afterthought, and that can result in lost sales and leads. Hire The Writing King to review your site and recommend changes to the text which will help communicate your message and improve your sales.

Blogging. Build engagement with your customers by hiring us to write a weekly or semi-weekly article for your blog, LinkedIn or other social media. Contact The Writing King today to discuss your blogging needs.

LinkedIn. LinkedIn is of the most important vehicles for finding new business, and a professionally written profile works to pulling in those leads. Write or update your profile today.

Technical Writing. We have broad experience in the computer, warehousing and retail industries, and have

Premium Writing Services

written hundreds of technical documents. Contact The Writing King today to find out how we can help you with your technical writing project.

The Writing King has the skills and knowledge to help you with any of your writing needs. Call us today to discuss how we can help you.